SOME FAMOUS IMAGES OF YORK
MOST PICTURES IN HERE YOU WILL SEE WHEN EXPLORING YORK.

SPIRIT OF
YORK

PAUL MOON

First published in Great Britain in 2009

British Library Cataloguing-in-Publication Data
A CIP record for this title is available from the British Library

ISBN 978 1 906887 35 3

PiXZ Books
Halsgrove House, Ryelands Industrial Estate,
Bagley Road, Wellington, Somerset TA21 9PZ
Tel: 01823 653777
Fax: 01823 216796
email: sales@halsgrove.com

An imprint of Halstar Ltd, part of the Halsgrove group of companies.
Information on all Halsgrove titles is available at: www.halsgrove.com

Printed and bound by Grafiche Flaminia, Italy

For Tina, Buddy, Simon, Andrew and Clare. X

Introduction

The city of York has always played a major role in the history of Great Britain. From the Roman legionaries who set up a garrison at the junction of the River Ouse and River Foss, through to the appointment of African Archbishop Dr John Sentamu, its residents have shared a spirited journey throughout the years.

This passage through time has been well preserved in York's stunning architecture and recorded through the exploits of its sons and daughters. A walk round the comparatively small city centre will take in Roman, Norman, Gothic, Tudor, Georgian, Victorian and modern day architecture, all stunning examples from these periods. Its glorious Cathedral, the Minster, is York's most impressive structure and dominates the skyline from all areas of the city and beyond. The medieval walls, with its four main gateways to the city centre, are some of the longest in the country and the Norman keep of Clifford's Tower is another outstanding example of York's impressive architectural heritage.

Tourists are spoilt for choice when they visit the city. The National Railway Museum, The Jorvik Viking Centre and the medieval timber-framed houses of Shambles; a leisurely boat trip on the River Ouse or an exhausting climb up the Minster's central tower. A day trip is never enough to take in all York has to offer.

The people of the city have left an indelible mark in the history books. Resident Roman emperors governed the whole of their substantial empire from York on two occasions; Viking and Norman kings used York to control the northern territories. From within the city walls Tudor and Stuart monarchs ran The Council of the North, and during the English Civil War Charles I was forced to move his family and court from London to York. In the nineteenth-century Victorian entrepreneurs and industrialists brought wealth and philanthropy for the needy population. Many other individuals have put the city firmly on the map including Guy Fawkes, St Margaret Clitherow and highwayman Dick Turpin.

In this spotlight on York I have showcased some of its classic tourist attractions as well as hidden highlights and some of the city's colourful characters and events, all of which contribute to making York one of the most exhilarating locations in England, if not the world, to visit.

Paul Moon

The author would like to thank the following: Churches Conservation Trust for Holy Trinity Church. York Minster for all Central Tower images. Kirkgate images by kind permission of York Museums Trust (York Castle Museum). York Castle Museum, York Art Galley and Yorkshire Museum images by kind permission of York Museums Trust. Ice Factor images by kind permission of Lunchbox Theatrical Productions. 'Accendo' created for Illuminating York 2008 by Ross Ashton – www.rossashton.com. Michael Mime aka Purpleman of York. Permissions were also sought for other images where necessary.

Right:

Bishopthorpe Palace, with its crystal clear reflection in the River Ouse, which is now the residence of Archbishop Dr John Sentamu. The palace has been home for York's archbishops for over 750 years.

Central Hall at the York University campus. The university was conceived in the 1960s and continues to be one of the leading educational institutes in the country.

Clifford's Tower. This Norman quatrefoil keep sits proud of its surroundings and offers excellent views across the city rooftops from its wall walk.

Above:
The keep of Clifford's Tower photographed from the steps of the County Court building that was built in the eighteenth century and designed by architect John Carr.

Right:
The statue of Roman Emperor Constantine that sits at the base of the Minster's South Transept. Constantine was declared emperor after his father's death in York in 306 AD.

Opposite:
Spring blossoms in the peaceful gardens of Dean's Park at the rear of the Minster.

Right:
The grassy banks on which the medieval walls of York sit are planted with millions of daffodil bulbs and these make a stunning display in early spring.

Autumn leaves cover the ground of Dean's Park with the Minster's West Towers visible through the trees.

The Victorian red brick building of the Dispensary on Duncombe Place. This was built to provide medicine and care for the expanding population who were prone to disease in the city slums.

The elaborate carved doorway of St Wilfrid's Catholic Church on Duncombe Place.
This short street offers a dramatic view of the Minster's West Towers.

Exhibition Square which is home to the City Art Gallery and King's Manor. This is a popular location for tourists to relax or catch a ride on one of the open top tour buses that circle the city centre.

The flooded River Ouse in Tower Park near Skeldergate Bridge. The Ouse carries vast quantities of rain that fall on the Yorkshire Dales and often bursts its banks in the city centre.

King's Staith under floodwater. Many of the houses and businesses along the banks of the Ouse have barriers installed due to the inevitable flooding.

Right:
The unique wooden pew boxes inside the hidden church of Holy Trinity. This wonderful church is run by the Churches Conservation Trust for tourists and visitors and does not hold any religious services.

The manor house of Heslington Hall in the grounds of York University. This building is now used for administration purposes by the university and students can relax in the peaceful gardens with their impressive topiary bushes.

The half stone and timber-framed Hospitium in the grounds of Museum Gardens. This building was a support building for St Mary's Abbey and is now used by York Museums Trust as a hospitality suite.

During winter months The Ice Factor sets up a temporary ice rink that is enjoyed by thousands of skaters. This sits in an area known as the Eye of York and is surrounded by York Castle Museum to the left and centre and the County Court building on the right. This elevated shot was taken from Clifford's Tower steps.

This curious construction near Monkgate Bar was a Victorian ice house. It has a deep pit that was filled with ice in winter for use throughout the summer.

King's Manor, which was originally built for the Abbot of St Mary's Abbey. It was used by Tudor and Stuart monarchs to run The Council of the North and became a Royalist stronghold during the English Civil War. The crest of Charles I sits above one of its doorways. The building is now used by York University as a campus.

King's Staith with a barge and pleasure boats moored on the Ouse while crowds enjoy an early evening drink outside the King's Arms public house.

The Victorian street of Kirkgate in Castle Museum. The street, named after the museum's founder, is a detailed recreation of shops and workshops from the nineteenth century and is staffed by costumed guides. The cobbled pavement was previously used as a prison courtyard before the building was converted to house the extensive collections of Dr John L. Kirk.

Lendal Tower and Lendal Bridge. The stone tower was used to hang a heavy chain across the Ouse to control river traffic in the middle ages. The Victorian iron bridge that spans the river was erected when the newly-built railway brought an influx of visitors and trade to the city.

Low Petergate. One of the busy shopping streets in the city centre offering views of the Minster's West Towers.

Stonegate leading to St Helen's Square with the Georgian-built Mansion House that is the residence of York's Lord Mayor.

Right:
Millennium Bridge.
The attractive curved cycle- and foot-bridge over the River Ouse joining Bishopthorpe Road to Fulford Road.

Above:
The War Memorial Gardens on Duncombe Place.
The elaborate monument was built as a memorial to local troops lost in South Africa during the Boer Wars.

Left:
The view of York Minster from Station Rise that is a popular location for photographic studies of the Minster.

Above:
One of the many carvings that adorn shops and houses around York. This attractive statuette is of Minerva, Roman goddess of wisdom, and was used by a bookseller to advertise his premises.

Right:
The view of the Minster's towers and South Transept from Deangate showing its impressive Gothic architecture.

Above:
The medieval walls on Station Rise. The walls stretch for over two miles round the city centre.

The elaborate flying buttresses and twin West Towers of the Minster. Viewed from the South Transept roof walk which leads to a steep spiral staircase up to the Central Tower viewpoint.

Right:
The West Towers of the Minster viewed from the Central Tower. Not recommended for vertigo sufferers!

The Minster from Station Rise at dusk when floodlights bathe the three towers.

The view towards the Minster from the walls of Clifford's Tower. In the foreground is the spire of York St Mary's Church with the lantern tower of All Saints' Church slightly obscured by tree branches.

The wider view of the city from Clifford's Tower walls showing Fairfax House, a Georgian town house regarded as one of the finest examples in the country.

The Roman Multangular Tower in the grounds of Museum Gardens, which formed part of the legionary fortress. The site is now surrounded by empty stone coffins.

Autumn in Museum Gardens with tree roots covered in fallen leaves. The botanical gardens offer a quiet retreat from the busy city centre and are home to many architectural gems including The Yorkshire Museum, St Mary's Abbey ruins, the Multangular Tower, The Hospitium and St Leonard's Hospital ruins.

The city centre open market on Newgate.

The Purpleman of York. This brightly coloured painted gentleman spends many hours in Stonegate making statuesque poses to the delight of shoppers and tourists, only stopping occasionally to rest and to pose for photographs. He has become something of a celebrity in the city.

The impressive architecture of the headquarters of North Eastern Railways (NER) built when York became a hub for the railways in the nineteenth century.

Left:
The Red House on Duncombe Place was originally a Georgian town house and is now a busy antiques centre.

Left:
Autumn colours reflected in the gently rippling River Ouse. This walkway along the river is called Dame Judi Dench Walk after the York-born actress.

Tourists take a relaxing cruise along the River Ouse. The river is only used for leisure vessels and by the York City Rowing Club.

Opposite:
The Rose Window on the South Transept of the Minster. This was destroyed in 1984 when lightning was believed to have started a fire in the transept roof.

Above:
A frosty morning in Rowntree's Park. The picturesque park was given by Rowntree and Company to the people of York as a memorial to staff who lost their lives in the First World War. It originally had a large outdoor swimming pool.

The Royal York Hotel that was built next to the second railway station after the first station became too small for the demands of trade and visitors. The new station, still in use, is one of England's finest with its curving platforms and dramatic roof arches.

The medieval cobbled street of Shambles at night. The overhanging timber-framed buildings were originally used by butchers to sell their wares. St Margaret Clitherow, who was pressed to death for harbouring Catholics in 1586, lived in one of the houses.

Skeldergate Bridge. Opened to the public in 1881, this was the third of York's bridges.
A toll was charged for crossing to recoup the cost of building.

St Helen's Square with the Mansion House at one end.
The square is also home to the famous Betty's Café Tea Rooms.

The impressive arched ceiling in the remains of St Leonard's Hospital in Museum Gardens. The Hospital was believed to have been the largest in medieval England.

Brickwork from St Mary's Abbey litters the grounds of Museum Gardens showing the extent of damage after the Dissolution of the Monasteries in 1536.

The busy attractive shopping street of Stonegate leading to the Minster.

St William's College, built for the Minster's Chantry Priests, is now a conference centre, restaurant and wedding reception location.

Opposite:
The city rooftops viewed from the Central Tower of York Minster.

Right:
Viewed from the Minster's Central Tower are the dominant structures of All Saints' Church lantern tower, York St Mary's Church spire and Clifford's Tower.

York has a strong Viking heritage and plays host to a yearly Viking Festival culminating in an evening battle re-enactment by hosts of authentically costumed Vikings. They form a rousing lengthy procession through the city streets before battling below Clifford's Tower in the Eye of York.

York's medieval walls in the springtime when the banks are blanketed in daffodils.

The pleasant walkway below the city walls on Lord Mayor's Walk in springtime.

The ornate carved stone porch on the West Door of the Minster.

Yorkshire Museum in the Museum Gardens, which houses many of York's archaeological treasures.

Left:
During the winter months of 2008 the Yorkshire Museum and St Mary's Abbey played host to 'Accendo', a stunning production of projected images and sounds, produced for Illuminating York in conjunction with Visit York.
The citywide event showcased various installations using light and sound to encourage visitors into the city centre.

Above:
York has many hidden passageways linking its main shopping streets. They are referred to locally as snickleways and this example, Lady Peckitt's Yard, is one of the finest, with views of the timber-framed house of traveller and historian Sir Thomas Herbert.

This attractive iron footbridge, known as the Blue Bridge, is at the junction of the Rivers Foss and Ouse.

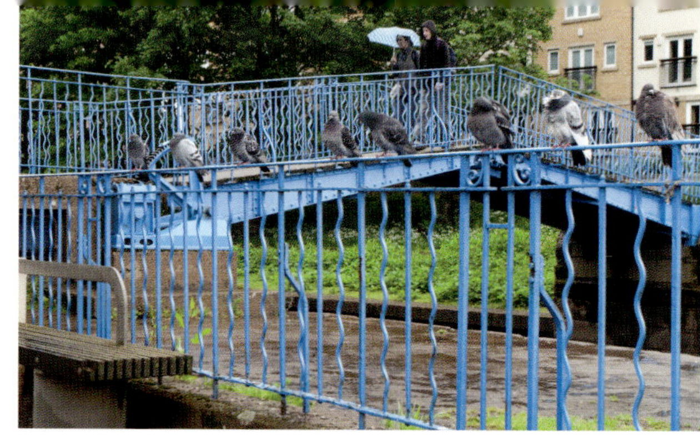

The strange carving of a red devil perched on a shop front in Stonegate. It was traditionally used by a printer to advertise his premises.